Vartuhy's Daughter

Cookbook of Family Favorites

by

Elizabeth Derderian

Compiled by
Janet Mrazek

Photographs & Illustrations by
Alison Derderian

Liz Derderian. . .

My mom is an amazing cook. Everything is made with love - whether it's a simple pork chop glazed with sweet and sour sauce or a time-intensive, multi-ingredient, traditional Armenian dish made with the intent that we come together as family and friends to enjoy the meal and each other. We were never allowed to leave for school without having a healthy breakfast. While breakfast foods may not have been my favorite, mornings were a great bonding experience as we kids sat there, staring into bowls of ever-expanding All-Bran, trying to figure out how the inch of cereal we poured into our bowls became large enough to dam the Mississippi River after milk was added. It also took decades, and the discovery of Hollandaise, to make my peace with poached eggs, but we never doubted the love behind each meal. Dinners, however, have been the best, and I swear no matter how many people there are at dinner, there is always enough food. Just the family – no problem. A surprise guest or three shows up – no problem. There is plenty to go around and always a place at the table. She is unfazeable.

One of my favorites is my mom's choreg. While eating them is certainly a treat, I love watching her make them. She has it down to a science, and before you know it, the morning-long process is over, and she is rolling the dough into perfect little braided rolls. I know this is one of my son's favorites as well. When he was little, it was a normal sight to find him up long before we were, sitting at the table with a choreg in each hand and mouth full. It's still his go-to breakfast when we're visiting, although he tries to keep it to one at a time these days! When I moved out on my own after college, my mom's gift to me was an Armenian cookbook (the orange one, of course) and an accordion folder, sectioned off by category and filled with recipes, both unique ones of my mom and ones handed down from my grandmother. I have added my own finds to the folder over the years but always find myself going to the original entries when I need a dish for a party or just for family dinner. While I still haven't mastered most of them, I keep trying! On my first attempt at making her choreg, my rolls were more lump than braid and were the taste and consistency of salted cannon balls, and my second attempt led to the rising dough escaping the bounds of its container and conquering my oven. Third time's the charm. I hope!

I am the lucky recipient of generations of experience. From my grandmother I learned that warm milk with sugar puts a child to sleep. From one of my aunts I learned that butter can live out on the counter without refrigeration. Disclaimer: I'm not brave enough to leave butter out on purpose, but when it's happened accidentally (this is me after all…), I don't panic and automatically throw it into the trash.

My mom had us helping in the kitchen for as long as I can remember. We started off as tiny sous chefs, stirring things, tearing lettuce and cleaning up spills, moved up to mid-sized line cooks responsible for individual dishes (I think pilaf was the first thing I learned to make on my own) and finally ended up as teenaged head chefs for a turn or two. My sister and brother were excellent students, so if you want an awesome meal, I have three houses in New England I can recommend!

Two of the best pieces of advice I ever got from Mom were that a good meal doesn't have to be fancy and complicated, and even if your meal doesn't come out the way you think it should, don't ever tell your guests. Chances are they will never notice unless you say something. While I know she's never had to use it, trust me, I've followed this second one a lot, and it works! Happy cooking!

Bethany Derderian Garabedian

Grape-nut Pudding

This book is dedicated to my father, Jim Derderian, who enjoyed nothing more than a warm bowl of grape-nut pudding. He would make it himself and carefully pour it into serving size bowls to share and always ordered it whenever it was on the menu at a restaurant. He would even choose grape-nut-flavored ice cream in the summertime. Here is the recipe so we all may experience the taste he loved so much.

Alison Derderian

Ingredients:

6 tablespoons grape-nut cereal

1/4 cup melted butter

1/2 cup sugar

3 beaten eggs

2 cups milk

1/4 cup raisins

1 teaspoon vanilla

1/8 teaspoon nutmeg

1/8 teaspoon cinnamon

1/8 teaspoon salt

Directions:

1. Mix grape-nut cereal and butter in large bowl.
2. Beat sugar and eggs together and add to the bowl.
3. Blend in milk, raisins, vanilla, salt and spices.
4. Pour into a one quart casserole and place in a pan with one inch water bath.
5. Cook in an oven at 375 for 5 minutes, stir and continue baking for 45 more minutes longer.
6. If making individual servings in one cup baking containers, adjust baking time.

Index of Recipes

APPETIZERS:

Cheese Boereg Bundt á la Azad 8
Hummus 9
Hot Artichoke Dip 10
Eetch 11
Tex Mex Dip 12

BREADS PLUS:

Blueberry Muffins 14
Bran Muffins 15
Choreg 16-17
Katah 18-19
Pecan Rolls 20
Popovers 21
Puffed Pancake with Strawberries 22
Pancakes 24

DESSERTS:

Apple Pie 26
Armenian Angel Cookies 27
Blueberry Cake 28
Blueberry Pie 29
Chocolate Chip Coffee Cake 30
Flan 31
Kadayiv with Cream Filling 32
Pecan Pie 33
Perfect Chocolate Cake 34
Scotcharoos á la Arpi 35
Paklava 36
Cream Puff Swans 37
Alison's Peanut Butter Cookies 38
Hot Fudge Sauce 39
Baked Alaska 40

Continued on next page

FISH AND MEAT:
Oven Baked Salmon 42

Beef Wellington 43

Oven Beef Stew 44

Luleh Kabob 45

Sini Kufte 46

GELATIN MOLDS:
Strawberry Gelatin Mold 48

Jellied Cranberry Mold 49

Mandarin Orange Salad 50

MISCELLANEOUS:
Grilled Cheese Sandwich 52

Pineapple Bread Stuffing 53

Strawberry Jam á la Jim 54

PILAFS AND PASTAS:
Cheese Noodle Dish 56

Bulghar Pilaf with Onions 57

Rice Pilaf 58

SALADS:
Spinach/Arugula Salad á la Shirley 60

Strawberry Spinach Salad 61

Baked Grapefruit Alaska. 62

Tomato Salad 63

Tropical Salad Bowl 64

SOUPS:
Red Lentil Soup 66

Lemon Egg Soup. 67

Roasted Chicken with Caramelized Onion Soup 68

Butternut Squash Soup. 69

Yogurt Noodle Soup 70

VEGETABLES:
Green Bean with Lamb 72

Green Beans with Olive Oil 73

Fresh Mushroom Casserole 74

Squash / Rice Dish. 75

PLANNING A DINNER PARTY 78

Appetizers

Bundt Pan Cheese Boereg á la Azad

Ingredients:

1 pound grated Muenster or Wisconsin Brick Cheese

1/2 pound cream cheese (8 oz)

2 eggs

1/4 cup chopped parsley

1-1/2 pounds phyllo dough

2 sticks unsalted butter

Topping:

2 eggs

1/2 cup milk

Directions:

1. Preheat oven to 375 degrees.
2. Rub the inside of a bundt pan with corn oil.
3. Chop parsley in blender and set aside.
4. Grate Muenster cheese in blender and set aside.
5. Beat 2 eggs in blender, add cream cheese.
6. In a large bowl, combine parsley, cheese and egg/cream cheese mixture.
7. Melt butter on stove or in microwave oven.
8. First layer: crinkle 3 phyllo dough, place next to each other to make a circle and brush with melted butter. Make a second and third layer like the first.
9. 4th layer: "spread" 1/2 of cheese mixture over 3rd layer.
10. 5th, 6th and 7th layer - same as first layer.
11. 8th layer: "spread" 1/2 of cheese mixture over 7th layer.
12. 9th, 10th and 11th layer - same as first layer.
13. Pour topping (2 eggs beaten with milk) over all.
14. Bake for 45 minutes or more until golden brown.

Hummus

Ingredients:

2 to 3 cloves garlic, peeled and hard tip removed

2 cups cooked chick-peas (if using canned chick peas, drain thoroughly)

1/3 cup tahini (sesame seed paste)

1 teaspoon salt, or to taste

3 tablespoons virgin olive oil

1/3 to 1/2 cup fresh lemon juice

Paprika and freshly chopped parsley to garnish

Pita bread and crudités to serve

Directions:

1. Using a food processor, turn motor on and drop garlic cloves, one at a time, through feed tube. Stop motor and remove cover.

2. Set aside 9 chick-peas for decoration.

3. Add remaining chick-peas, tahini, and salt. Cover and process a few seconds.

4. Add oil and lemon juice through feed tube with motor running. Process until smooth, scraping down sides of bowl as needed. Adjust seasoning.

5. Spread on serving platter. Place 3 reserved chick-peas in center of platter and 3 on each side of platter as shown on page 7. Sprinkle with paprika and garnish with chopped parsley. Additional olive oil can be poured over hummus when served, if desired. Served with pita bread or crudités.

6. Hummus can be covered and stored in refrigerator up to one week.

Note: Hummus is very versatile. Here hummus is garnished with avocado and green hemp oil.

Hot Artichoke Dip

Ingredients:

2 (14 oz) cans artichoke hearts - drained, squeezed and finely chopped

1/2 teaspoon garlic powder

8 green onion tops - chopped

12 oz sliced bacon - cooked and crumbled

1 cup grated Parmesan cheese

1/2 cup mayonnaise

Paprika

Directions:

1. Preheat oven to 350 degrees.
2. Mix artichoke hearts, garlic powder, onions, bacon, cheese and mayonnaise.
3. Place in 2 quart ovenproof dish.
4. Bake uncovered 20 minutes.
5. Sprinkle with paprika.
6. Serve with tortilla chips, corn chips or crackers.

Eetch

Ingredients:

1 cup fine bulghar

15 oz can ground peeled tomatoes (puree)

1/2 cup corn oil

1/2 cup lemon juice

1 chopped green pepper

1 chopped red onion

1/2 cup chopped parsley

1 teaspoon dried mint

1 teaspoon salt

1/4 teaspoon pepper

Directions:

1. Mix all ingredients and refrigerate overnight.
2. Before serving mix again (fluff) to loosen mixture.
3. Garnish with parsley and lemon slices.
4. Serve with Syrian bread or Romaine lettuce.

Tex Mex Dip

Ingredients:

3 medium avocados

2 tablespoons lemon juice

1/2 teaspoons salt

1/2 teaspoon pepper

1 cup sour cream

1/2 cup mayonnaise

1 package (3 oz.) taco seasoning

2 cans (15 oz each) bean dip

1 large bunch scallions with tops, chopped

3 medium tomatoes - chopped and seeded

2 cans (3.5 oz) pitted ripe olives coarsely chopped

1 package (8 oz) shredded sharp cheddar cheese

Directions:

1. Peel, pit and mash avocados with lemon juice, salt and pepper.
2. Combine sour cream, mayonnaise and taco seasoning in a bowl.
3. Layer the ingredients as shown here. First spread bean dip on shallow serving platter.
4. Layer with avocado mixture on top of the bean layer.
5. Layer the sour cream mixture on top of the avocado layer.
6. Sprinkle with chopped onions, tomatoes and olives.
7. Cover with shredded cheese.
8. Serve with tortilla or your favorite chips.

Breads Plus

Blueberry Muffins

Ingredients for cake:

3 cups flour

1-1/2 cups sugar

2 teaspoons baking powder

1/2 teaspoon salt

2 eggs

1 cup milk

1/3 cup vegetable oil

1/2 teaspoon vanilla

2 cups fresh or frozen blueberries

Directions:

1. Preheat oven to 400 degrees.
2. Spray oil on extra large muffin tins.
3. Mix flour, sugar, baking powder and salt in a large bowl.
4. Combine eggs, milk, oil and vanilla and add to the dry mixture.
5. Fold in blueberries.
6. Spoon batter into muffin cups 2/3 full.
7. Sprinkle sugar on each muffin.
8. Bake 20 minutes or until golden on top and center is baked.

Bran Muffins

Ingredients:

4 eggs

1 quart buttermilk

1 cup oil

2 cups sugar

1/2 cup honey

5 cups flour

5 teaspoons baking soda

1-1/2 teaspoons salt

7-1/2 cups raisin bran cereal

1 cup seedless raisins

Directions:

1. Beat eggs.
2. Add buttermilk, oil, sugar and honey and mix all together.
3. Add flour, baking soda, salt, and cereal mixing well.
4. Add in raisins.
5. Spray large muffin tins with cooking oil.
6. Spoon in batter 2/3 full and sprinkle with sugar.
7. Bake at 400 degrees for 15-20 minutes. Complete recipe makes 24 large muffins.

Note: Batter will keep 3-4 weeks in the refrigerator.

Choreg

Ingredients:

6-7 cups flour

1 cup sugar

1 teaspoon baking powder

1 teaspoon salt

1 tablespoon mahleb

5 eggs

2 sticks butter (in 2 cup measuring cup)

1 cup milk

5 teaspoons yeast in 1/2 cup warm water with a dash of sugar

Directions:

1. Turn oven to 200 degrees to warm slightly and turn off. Turn on oven light for continued warmth.
2. In large pan mix 6-7 cups flour with sugar, baking powder, salt, and mahleb.
3. In a separate medium sized bowl beat 5 eggs.
4. Melt 2 sticks butter (in 2 cup measuring cup) and add enough milk to make 2 cups.
5. Mix yeast in warm water with a dash of sugar and let sit for five minutes in a small bowl.
6. Add butter mixture, yeast and eggs to dry ingredients.
7. Knead lightly – add flour if needed.
8. Oil dough and sides of pan. Place dough in pan and cover and place in oven for 3 hours to rise.
9. Remove dough from pan onto floured surface. Divide into about 32-36 balls. Shape and put on parchment covered cookie sheets.
10. Cover with cloth and let rise for 1 hour.
11. Brush choregs with 1 beaten egg and one egg yolk mixed with 1/4 teaspoon sugar.
12. Sprinkle with sesame seeds.
13. Bake for 13 to 15 minutes in a 375 degree oven until brown.
14. Cool on a rack.

> She would make the most delicious things! I remember coming home from school and the whole house smelling like fresh, hot choreg!

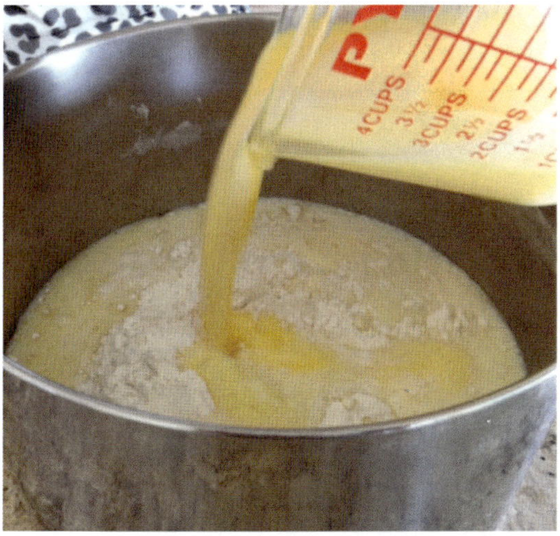
4CUPS
3½
3CUPS
2½
2CUPS
1½
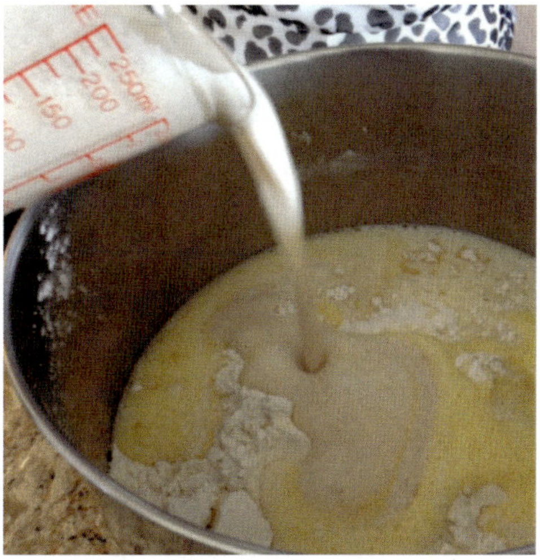
250ml
200
150
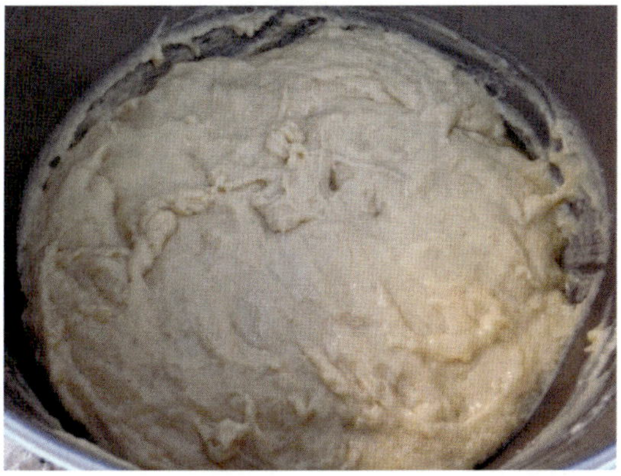
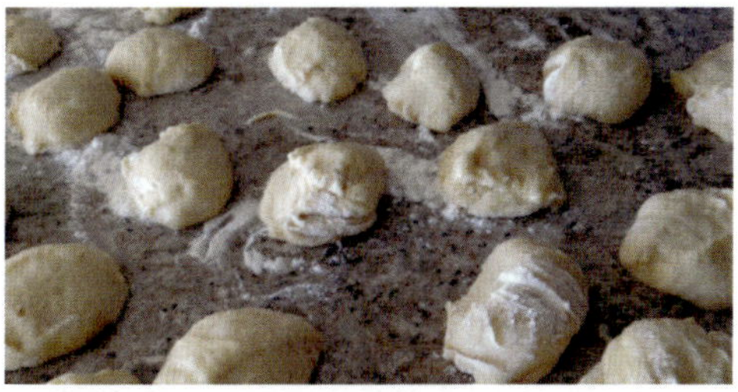
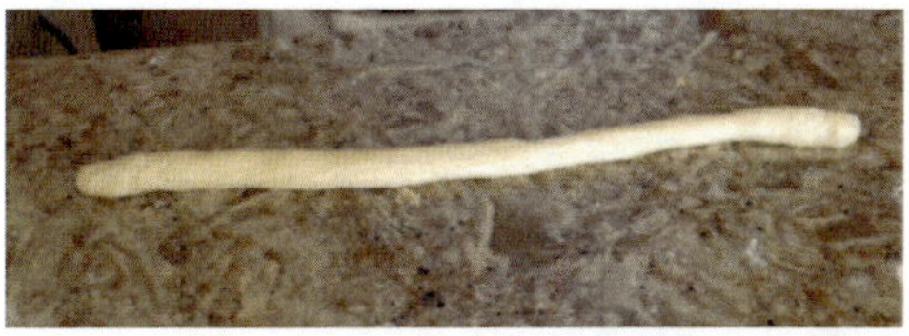
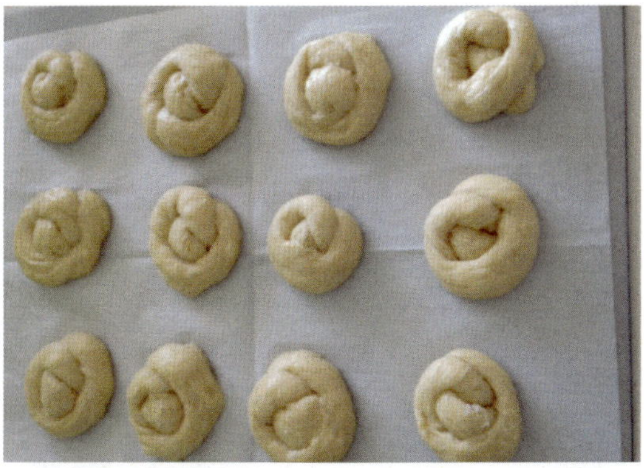
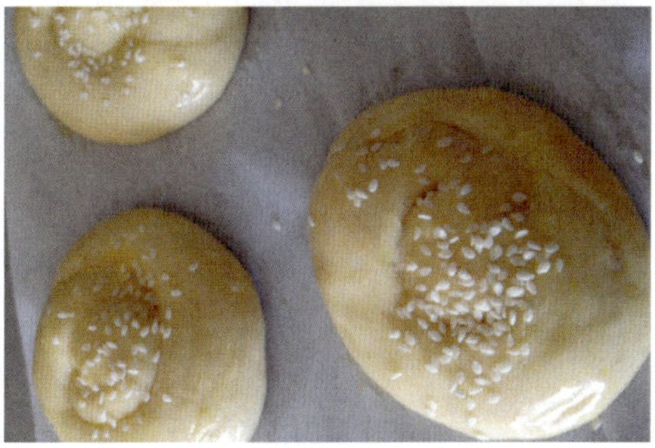
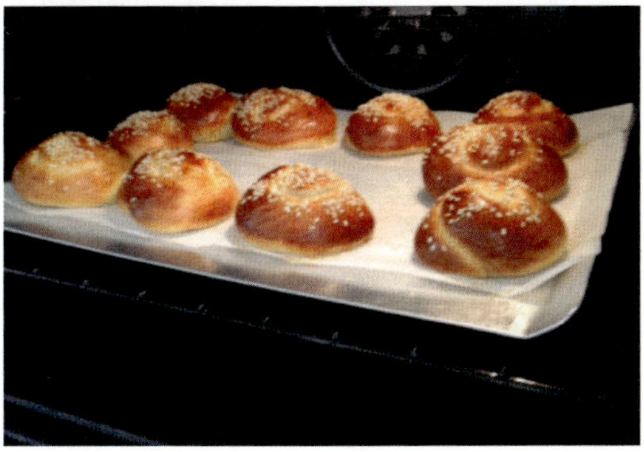
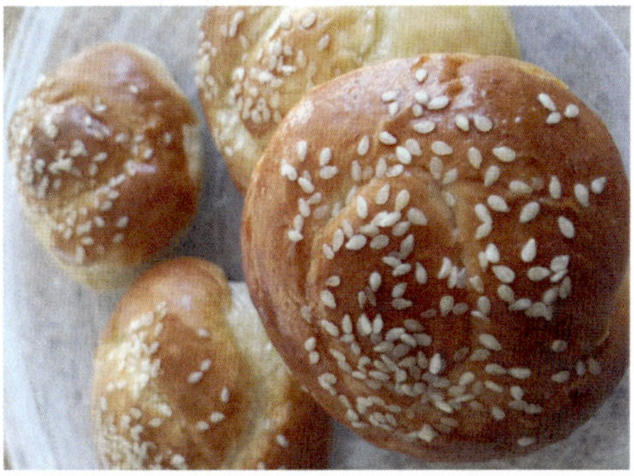

Katah

Ingredients:

7-10 cups flour

3 teaspoons baking powder

1/2 teaspoons salt

3/4 cup sugar

4 beaten eggs

2 packages (.25 oz each) dry yeast

1/2 cup warm water

1/2 teaspoon sugar

1/2 cup shortening

1/2 cup butter

1 cup whole milk

1 cup evaporated milk

Directions:

1. In a large bowl mix 7 cups of flour, salt, sugar and baking powder.
2. In a separate bowl beat eggs.
3. Mix together yeast, warm water and 1/2 teaspoon of sugar.
4. Stir and set aside to proof (until double).
5. Melt and clarify shortening and butter.
6. Warm whole milk and evaporated milk.
7. Warm oven to 200 degrees and then turn off.
8. Add 1/4 cup melted butter and shortening mixture to the flour, continue adding milk mixture, yeast mixture and eggs to the flour.
9. Knead until dough is smooth and elastic.
10. Oil bowl and turn dough to oil surface.
11. Cover and place in the warm oven.
12. Let rise until double in bulk (2-3 hours).
13. Divide dough into balls (6 to 9) and place on a floured surface and cover with cloth for 20 minutes.
14. Roll each ball into a large thin circle.
15. Brush each circle with melted butter/shortening mixture.
16. Cut each circle in half, place one half on top of the other and roll up, jellyroll fashion, starting with the straight edge.
17. Wind the roll into a concentric circle.
18. Set aside 10 minutes, then flatten slightly with hands or rolling pin.
19. Place on a baking sheet, cover with cloth and let rise 1 hour.
20. Brush top with beaten egg. Sprinkle sesame seeds if desired.
21. Bake in preheated 375 degree oven 20 minutes on lower rack and 10 minutes on upper rack until golden.

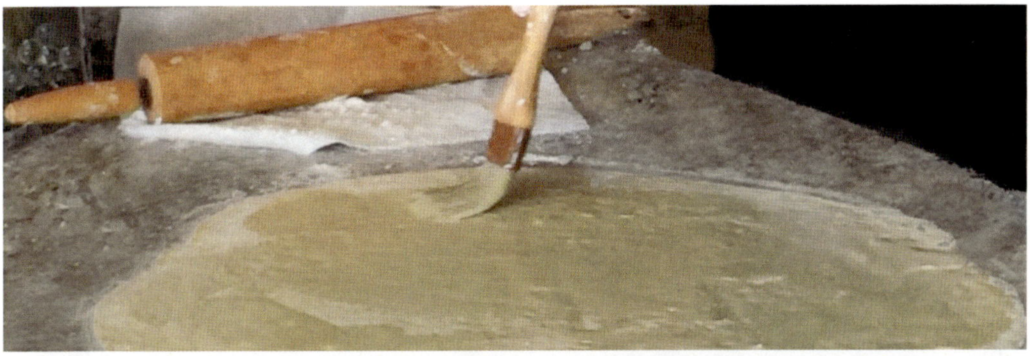
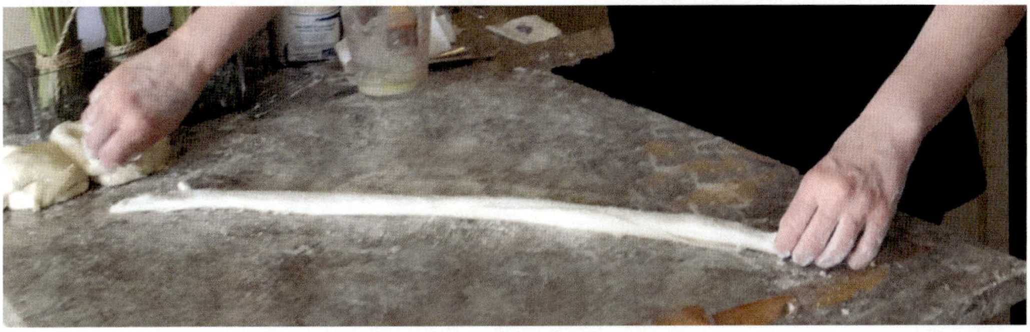
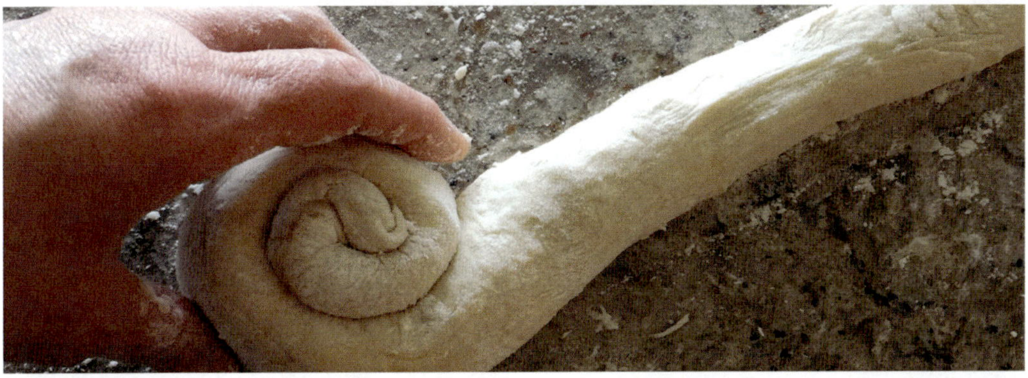
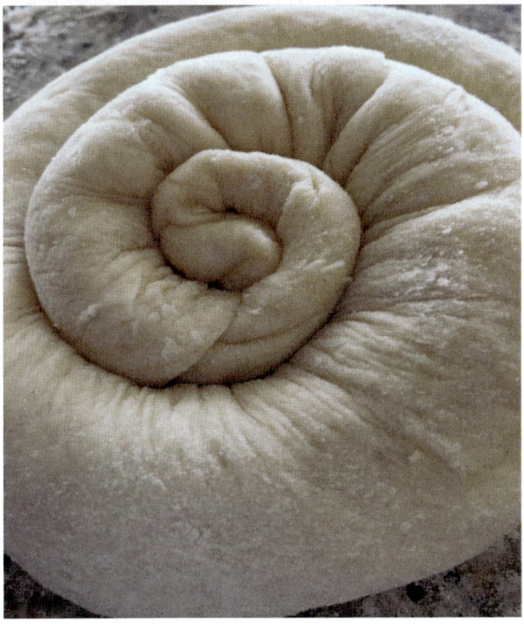
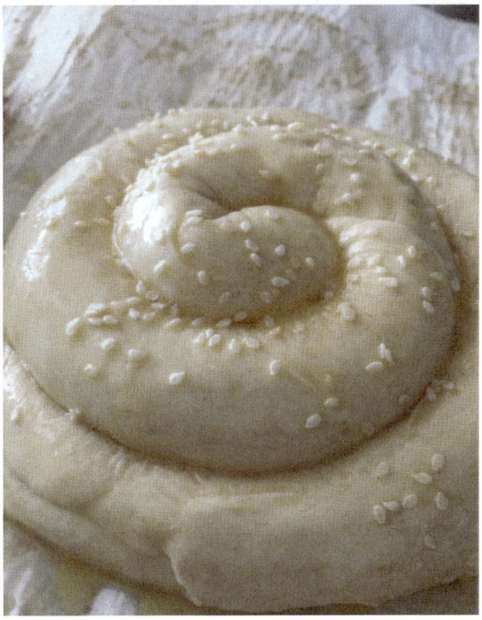

Pecan Rolls

Ingredients:

1 cup milk

1/4 cup butter

1 egg

1/4 cup sugar

1 teaspoon salt

1 package (.25 oz) dry yeast

3-1/2 to 4 cups flour

Topping

1/4 cup butter

1/4 cup brown sugar

1 tablespoon maple syrup

1/2 cup pecans or walnuts

Filling

1/4 cup sugar

1 teaspoon cinnamon

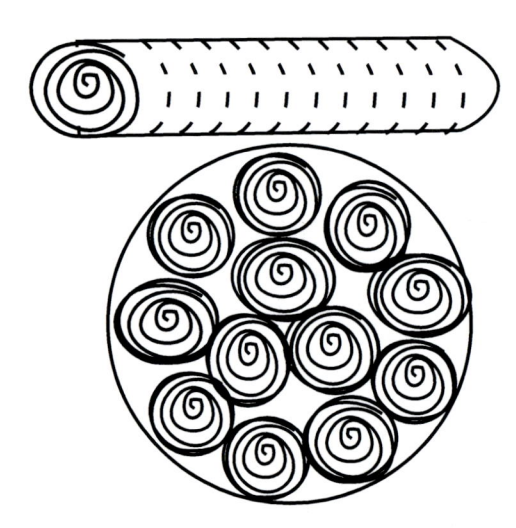

Directions:

1. Heat milk & butter.
2. Pour into mixing bowl.
3. Add egg, sugar, salt, yeast and 2 cups of flour.
4. Beat 2 minutes with electric beater.
5. Gradually add remaining flour by hand until no longer sticks to side of bowl.
6. Knead dough until nice soft dough forms.
7. Place in bowl greased with corn oil. Place in warm place to double in size. about 2-3 hours.
8. Heat topping ingredients.
9. Pour 1/2 of mixture into each of two 8" round cake pans.
10. Sprinkle each with half of nuts.
11. Punch down dough, remove from bowl and cut into 2 pieces.
12. Roll each into a 9 x 12 rectangle.
13. Sprinkle each piece with half the filling.
14. Roll up tightly into a 12 inch long roll.
15. Cut into twelve 1 inch pieces and place in cake pan evenly spaced.
16. Cover and let rise until double in size, 2-3 hours.
17. Bake in preheated 375 degree oven 20 to 25 minutes.
18. Remove immediately from pan and cool on rack.

Popovers

Ingredients:

4 eggs

2 cups milk

2 cups flour

1 teaspoon salt

Directions:

1. Heat oven to 450 degrees.
2. Spray popover pans with oil.
3. Place ingredients in a blender and blend until smooth.
4. Fill popover pans 2/3 full.
5. Bake 20 minutes at 450 degrees, turn down oven temperature to 350 degrees and bake 15 to 20 minutes until golden brown.
6. Remove from pan immediately and serve hot.

Puffed Pancakes with Strawberries

Ingredients:

6 eggs

1 cup milk

1/4 cup orange juice

1/2 cup sugar

1 cup flour

1/4 teaspoon salt

1/4 lb butter

Strawberry Sauce (recipe to follow)

Powdered sugar, if desired

Dairy sour cream, if desired

Ingredients for Strawberry Sauce

2 (10-oz.) pkgs. Frozen strawberries in syrup

2 tablespoons orange juice

Directions:

1. In a blender mix eggs, milk, orange juice, sugar, flour and salt until blended.
2. Preheat oven to 425 degrees.
3. Melt butter in a 13" x 9" baking dish in oven until it sizzles but not brown.
4. Remove baking dish from oven and immediately pour batter into sizzling butter.
5. Bake in middle of oven 20 minutes or until puffed and brown.
6. While pancake is baking heat strawberries in microwave oven until thawed and slightly warm and stir in orange juice.
7. Remove pancake from oven.
8. Sprinkle with powdered sugar.
9. Pancake falls quickly so serve immediately with warm Strawberry Sauce and sour cream.

My Mother's Hands

My mother's hands have soothed the brows
Of three small fevered heads.
And countless times have tucked three chins
With blankets in their beds.
They've wiped crocodile tears, quelled silly fears
And turned pages of magical fables.
They've bandaged scraped knees, so tenderly,
And set such pretty holiday tables.
And what we recall, most fondly of all,
Are the delights she would make with those hands.
Pies, cookies and cakes, oh, that rich chocolate cake!
Most coveted cake in the land.
Shaping choreg with ease, we'd cry out, "Yes, Please!"
And her hand placed one on a plate.
We'd dip pieces with pride,
In some jam on the side,
A warm treat that was well worth the wait.
My mother's hands have had many roles.
They've filled our tummies and our souls.
They've lifted us higher than we thought we could reach,
And even today, they continue to teach,
With Love, Generosity, Kindness and Grace,
In my mother's hands,
I see a beautiful place.

by Alison Derderian

Pancakes

Ingredients:

1 egg

1/2 cup plain yogurt

1/2 cup milk

2 tablespoons salad oil

1 cup flour

2 tablespoons sugar

1 teaspoon baking powder

1/2 teaspoon baking soda

1/2 teaspoon salt

Directions:

1. Beat egg.

2. Add yogurt, milk and salad oil.

3. Add remaining ingredients and mix.

4. Ladle about 1/4 cup of batter onto medium-high temperature grill sprayed with cooking oil. Make the pancakes into shapes or letters of the alphabet to delight your children!

5. When pancake forms bubbles on top turn and cook other-side of pancake.

Saturday mornings were for pancakes!
(And not just any pancakes!)

Desserts

Apple Pie

Ingredients:

Double Crust Pastry (Recipe on page 33)

1/2 cup sugar

1/3 cup packed brown sugar

2 tablespoons flour

1/2 teaspoon ground cinnamon

1/4 teaspoon ground nutmeg

1/4 teaspoon salt

2 tablespoons butter

7 cups thinly sliced peeled apples

1 tablespoon sugar

1/8 teaspoon of cinnamon

Directions:

1. Prepare dough for pastry. Refrigerate.
2. Combine 1/2 cup sugar, brown sugar, flour, cinnamon, nutmeg and salt in a small bowl.
3. Cut in butter until pieces are the size of large peas.
4. Place apple slices in a large bowl.
5. Add sugar mixture and toss to coat apples.
6. Preheat oven to 375 degrees.
7. Cut dough in 2 equal portions.
8. On a lightly floured surface, roll out 1 portion to an 11" circle.
9. Fit into a 9" pie pan.
10. Spoon apple mixture into unbaked pie shell.
11. Trim edge of dough to rim of pan.
12. Roll out remaining dough to a 12" circle.
13. Cut slits as desired and fit circle over filling.
14. Fold top edge under bottom edge, making a raised edge and flute as desired.
15. Glaze as desired or combine 1 tablespoon sugar and 1 teaspoon cinnamon and sprinkle over pie.
17. Cover edge with foil and bake 25 minutes.
18. Remove foil and bake 25 to 30 minutes longer until crust is golden brown, apples are tender and juices are bubbly.

Armenian Angel Cookies

Ingredients:

1 pound sweet butter

4 cups sifted cake flour

10 tablespoons powdered sugar plus powdered sugar for sifting over baked cookies

1 teaspoon vanilla

2 cups finely chopped pecans or walnuts

2 egg yolks

Directions:

1. Beat butter for 10 minutes.
2. Add sugar.
3. Add flour, vanilla, nuts, egg yolks.
4. Roll in balls and flatten to the size of a nickle.
5. Bake at 325 degrees for about 20 minutes.
6. Sift powdered sugar on top of baked cookies.

Makes 100 cookies.
Note: Photo of baked cookies appear on page 25.

Blueberry Cake

Ingredients for cake:

3 cups flour

2 cups sugar

2 teaspoons baking powder

1 teaspoon salt

2 eggs

1 cup milk

1/3 cup vegetable oil

1/2 teaspoon vanilla

2 cups fresh or frozen blueberries

Ingredients for Topping:

1/4 teaspoon nutmeg

1/4 cup sugar

Directions:

1. Preheat oven to 350 degrees.
2. Grease and flour a 9 x 13 inch pan.
3. Sift flour, 2 cups sugar, baking powder and salt in a large bowl.
4. Combine eggs, milk, oil and vanilla and add to the dry mixture, mixing well.
5. Fold in blueberries.
6. Put into pan.
7. Sprinkle topping over cake batter.
8. Bake 50 minutes or until golden on top.

Blueberry Pie

Ingredients:

Double Pastry Crust (Recipe on page 33)

3/4 cup sugar

2 tablespoons quick-cooking tapioca

1/4 teaspoon salt

1 teaspoon finely shredded lemon peel

5 to 6 cups blueberries

Directions:

1. Prepare dough for crust and refrigerate.
2. Combine sugar, tapioca and salt in a medium bowl.
3. Add lemon peel and blueberries.
4. Toss to coat berries with sugar mixture.
5. Preheat oven to 375 degrees.
6. Cut dough in 2 equal portions.
7. On a lightly floured surface, roll out 1 portion to an 11" circle.
8. Fit into a 9" pan and trim edge of dough to rim of pan.
9. Spoon blueberry mixture into unbaked pie shell.
10. Roll out remaining dough to a 12" circle.
11. Cut slits as desired and fit circle over filling.
12. Fold top edge under bottom edge, making a raised edge.
13. Flute as desired.
14. Glaze and top as desired.
15. Cover edge with foil and bake 25 minutes.
16. Remove foil and bake 20 to 25 minutes longer until crust is golden brown and juices are bubbly.

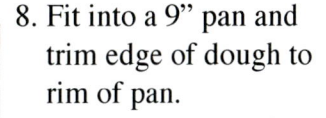

Chocolate Chip Coffee Cake

Ingredients:

Pecan Topping:

1/4 cup sugar

1 teaspoon cinnamon

1/4 cup chopped pecans

Cake:

1/4 pound butter (1 stick at room temperature)

1 (8 oz) package cream cheese (room temperature)

1 cup sugar

2 eggs

1 teaspoon vanilla extract

2 cups flour

1 teaspoon baking powder

1/2 teaspoon baking soda

1/4 teaspoon salt

1/4 cup cold milk

1 (6 oz) package chocolate chips (1 cup)

Directions:

1. Preheat oven to 350 degrees.
2. Grease a 9" x 3" springform pan and set aside.
3. Mix ingredients for pecan topping and set aside.
4. In a large bowl, cream butter, cream cheese and sugar.
5. Add eggs 1 at a time, beating well after each addition.
6. Add vanilla, flour, baking powder, baking soda and salt; mix well.
7. Stir in cold milk and chocolate chips. Mixture will be very thick.
8. Pour into prepared pan.
9. Sprinkle with Pecan Topping.
10 Bake 55 to 60 minutes or until wooden pick inserted in the center comes out clean.
11. Let cool 15 minutes.
12. Remove outside ring from springform pan and cool cake completely.

Flan

Ingredients:

Syrup

3/4 cup sugar

Custard

2 cups milk

2 cups light cream

6 eggs, slightly beaten

1/2 cup sugar

1/2 teaspoon salt

2 teaspoons vanilla extract

Boiling water

Directions:

1. Preheat oven to 350 degrees.
2. Carefully heat sugar in a large heavy skillet, cooking over medium heat until sugar melts and forms a light brown syrup.
3. Immediately pour syrup into heated 9 inch round shallow baking dish.
4. Turn pan to coat bottom and sides and set aside.
5. In medium saucepan heat milk and cream just until bubbles form around edge of pan. (This can also be heated in a 4 cup measuring cup in the microwave oven for 4 minutes.)
6. In large bowl, combine eggs, sugar, salt and vanilla.
7. Gradually stir in hot milk mixture.
8. Pour into prepared dish.
9. Set dish in shallow pan; pour boiling water to 1/2 inch depth around dish.
10. Bake 45-60 minutes or until knife inserted in center comes out clean.
11. Let custard cool; refrigerate 4 hours or overnight.
12. To serve, run small spatula around edge of dish to loosen.
13. Invert on shallow serving dish, shaking gently to release. The caramel acts as a sauce.

Kadayiv with Cream Filling

Ingredients:

Simple Syrup:

2 cups sugar

1 cup water

1 tablespoon lemon juice

Kadayiv:

1 pound shredded kadayiv dough, buy at Middle eastern grocery store

2 sticks melted unsalted butter

Cream Filling:

4 cups light cream

1/4 cup cornstarch

1/8 teaspoon vanilla powder or extract

4 tablespoons sugar

Directions:

For Simple Syrup:

1. Dissolve sugar and water together in pan and cook for 10 minutes. Place paper towel over pan while cooking to avoid splatter.
2. Add lemon juice, cool and refrigerate.

For Kadayiv:

1. Pull Kadayiv apart with hands in large bowl.
2. Add melted butter to shredded dough set aside.
3. Make cream filling: cook cream with cornstarch. Add vanilla and sugar and cook until it is the consistency of pudding. Cool.
4. Divide Kadayiv mixture in half.
5. Pat half of dough evenly into a buttered 9 x 12 baking dish.
6. Spread COOLED cream filling over bottom layer.
7. Top with remaining dough and pat down.
8. Bake 350 degrees until light brown 45 to 55 minutes.

Pecan Pie

Ingredients for double crust:

2 cups flour

1 teaspoons salt

1/4 cup butter

1/2 cup shortening

1/2 cup cold water

Filling

1 unbaked pie shell

3 eggs

1/2 cup sugar

1 cup dark corn syrup

1/8 teaspoon salt

1 teaspoon vanilla

1/4 cup oil

1 cup pecans

Directions

Note: Pie crust recipe makes two crusts. You need only one crust for Pecan Pie.

1. Stir flour and salt together in a medium bowl.
2. With pastry blender cut in shortening and butter until pieces are the size of small peas.
3. Gradually add water and toss with a fork until all flour is moistened and mixture starts to form a ball.
4. If necessary, add more flour to crumbs in bottom of bowl.
5. Gather dough in your hands, divide into 2 balls and gently shape into flat balls.
6. Roll out one round ball and place in the bottom of a pie plate. Save other ball for another use.
7. Beat eggs and add all ingredients except pecans.
8. Cover bottom of pie crust with pecans.
9. Pour mixture over pecans.
10. Bake at 350 degrees for 1 hour.

Perfect Chocolate Cake

Ingredients:
Filling
1 cup heavy cream chilled
1/4 cup unsifted confectioners' sugar
1 teaspoon vanilla extract

Cake
1 cup unsweetened cocoa
2 cups boiling water
2-3/4 cups sifted (sift before measuring) flour
2 teaspoons baking soda
1/2 teaspoon salt
1/2 teaspoon baking powder
1 cup butter, softened
2-1/2 granulated sugar
4 eggs
1-1/2 teaspoons vanilla extract

Frosting
1 package (6 oz.) semi-sweet chocolate chips
1/2 cup light cream
1 cup butter
2-1/2 cups unsifted confectioners' sugar

Directions-Cake:
1. In medium bowl combine unsweetened cocoa with 2 cups boiling water, mixing until smooth.
2. Cool completely.
3. Sift flour with soda, salt and baking powder.
4. Preheat oven to 350 degrees.
5. Cut waxed paper to fit each of the bottoms of three 9" layer cake pans.
6. Spray each pan with cooking oil.
7. In large bowl of electric mixer at high speed, beat butter, sugar, eggs and vanilla until light and fluffy - about 5 minutes.
8. At low speed, beat in the flour mixture (in fourths) alternating with cocoa mixture. (in thirds).
9. Begin and end with flour mixture. Do not overbeat.
10. Divide evenly into pans and smooth tops with spatula.
11. Bake 25 to 30 minutes or until surface springs back when gently pressed with fingertip.
12. Cool in pans 10 minutes.
13. Loosen sides with spatula and remove cakes from pans and cool on racks.

Filling
1. Whip cream with sugar and vanilla.
2. On cake serving plate, place a layer, top side down and spread with half of cream mixture.
3. Place 2nd layer top side down and spread with rest of cream mixture.
4. Place 3rd layer top side up.

Frosting
1. In medium saucepan combine chocolate chips, cream, and butter and stir over medium heat until smooth.
2. Remove from heat and blend in confectioners' sugar.
3. Turn into bowl and place over ice and beat until frosting holds shape.
4. With metal spatula, frost sides first covering whipped cream.
5. Frost top of cake swirling to decorate. Refrigerate 1 hour.

Scotcharoos á la Arpi

Ingredients:

1 cup sugar

1 cup corn syrup

1 cup peanut butter

6 cups Rice Krispies

1 cup semi-sweet chocolate chips

1 cup butterscotch chips

Directions:

1. Butter 9 x 12 glass baking dish.

2. Melt sugar and corn syrup in 8 cup measuring bowl in microwave for 4 minutes.

3. Stir in peanut butter and Rice Krispies.

4. Press into baking dish.

5. Mix chocolate and butterscotch chips together in glass bowl and microwave for 2 minutes.

6. Spread over Rice Krispie mixture.

7. When cool, cut into squares.

Paklava

Ingredients for Simple Syrup:

(About 12 x 18 pan)

2 cups water

3 cups sugar

2 teaspoon lemon juice

Ingredients for Filling:

5 cups ground walnuts

2 teaspoon cinnamon

4 tablespoon sugar

Ingredients for Dough:

2 packages (1 lb each) of phyllo dough

2 pounds unsalted butter (maybe more)

Directions for Simple Syrup:

1. Boil water and sugar together for 10 min.
2. Remove from heat
3. Stir in lemon juice and refrigerate

Directions for Filling:

1. Mix nuts cinnamon and sugar and set aside.

Directions:

1. Melt butter in measuring cup in microwave about 3 sticks at a time.
2. Brush bottom of pan with melted butter and lay first sheet in pan and brush with melted butter.
3.
4. Continue until finished with 1 pound of dough.
5. Spread walnut mixture. Sprinkle some melted butter directly over walnuts.
6. Continue layering 2nd pound of phyllo dough brushing melted butter in between each layer.
7. Cover and refrigerate a few hours.
8. Remove from refrigerator and cut into diamond shapes using a serrated knife.
9. Bake for 15 minutes in 400 degree oven.
10. Reduce heat to 325 degrees and bake 30 to 40 minutes until golden color.
11. Turn oven off but leave paklava in oven for another 10 minutes.
12. Remove from oven and pour on cold syrup.
13. Cool about 2 hours, recut and store loosely covered at room temperature.

Cream Puff Swans

Ingredients for Cream Puff:

1 cup milk

1 stick of butter

1 teaspoon sugar

Dash of salt

1 cup flour

4 large eggs

1 quart plus 1 pint vanilla ice cream

Ingredients for Fudge Sauce:

2 sticks butter

1 (12 oz.) package chocolate chips

1 cup coarsely chopped walnuts or pecans

Directions for sauce:

1. In a double boiler over hot water melt butter and chocolate chips, stirring until smooth.
2. Stir in nuts.
3. Serve hot. May be refrigerated and reheated.

Directions for Cream Puff:

1. In a medium sauce pan over medium heat, heat milk, butter, sugar, and salt only until mixture begins to boil and butter is melted.
2. Remove from heat and immediately pour in flour.
3. Stir vigorously until dough forms a ball and leaves the sides of the pan.
4. Return to heat and stir 1-2 minutes to dry out dough.
5. Remove from heat and make a well in center and add eggs one at a time, beating after each one.
6. After the last one, beat one minute until dough is shiny and smooth.
7. Preheat oven to 400 degrees and lightly grease 2 baking sheets.
8. Fill a pastry bag with a 5/8" rose tip, using 1/4 of batter and pipe out 12-14 swan necks.
9. To make bodies, drop 2 1/2 " balls of dough on the second cookie sheet.
10. Bake bodies 25-30 minutes, cool in oven with door ajar for one hour. Bake necks 10 minutes and remove from oven.

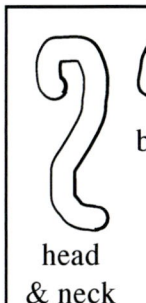

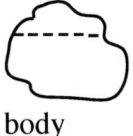

head & neck   body   wings

TO ASSEMBLE:
Cut the top third of each baked body. Cut that top in half to make the wings. Fill the bottom with icecream. Insert one end of the neck in the ice cream and the wings on each side of the body.

Alison's Peanut Butter Cookies

Ingredients:

1/2 cup butter

1/2 cup peanut butter

1/2 cup sugar

1/2 cup brown sugar

1 egg

1/2 teaspoon vanilla

1 1/4 cups sifted flour

3/4 teaspoon baking soda

1/4 teaspoon salt

Directions

1. Beat the butter until creamy, 2 minutes.
2. Add brown sugar and white sugar and beat for 2 more minutes.
3. Mix in the peanut butter and the egg.
4. In a separate bowl vigorously whisk together the dry ingredients: flour, baking soda, and salt.
5. Stir the dry ingredients into the sugar butter mixture.
6. Wrap dough in plastic and refrigerate at least 3 hours.
7. Preheat oven to 375 degrees. Shape the dough into 1 1/4 inch balls.
9. Place 3 inches apart on ungreased cookie sheets. Flatten in a criss cross pattern with a fork. and bake for 8 minutes.
10. Add dark chocolate and pinch of salt immediately after removing from oven. Chocolate and salt will melt into the criss crosses creating a delightful mouthful of decadence.

Hot Fudge Sauce

Ingredients:

2/3 cup heavy cream

1/2 cup light corn syrup

1/3 cup dark brown sugar

1/4 cup unsweetened dutch processed cocoa powder

1/4 teaspoon salt

3 oz fine quality bittersweet chocolate, finely chopped

2 tablespoons unsalted butter

1 teaspoon vanilla

Directions:

1. Bring first 5 ingredients to a boil.
2. Reduce heat and low boil for 5 minutes.
3. Remove from heat and add butter, vanilla and remaining chocolate.
4. Mix until smooth.

Baked Alaska

Ingredients:

2 quarts peppermint stick ice cream, softened

1 (18.25 oz) package chocolate cake mix

1/2 teaspoon almond extract

8 egg whites

1/8 teaspoon cream of tartar

1/8 teaspoon salt

1 cup white sugar

Directions:

1. Line the bottom and sides of an 8-inch round mixing bowl with foil. Spread ice cream in bowl, packing firmly. Cover and freeze 8 hours or until firm.

2. Preheat oven to 350 degrees. Grease and flour two 9" round cake pan.

3. Prepare cake mix according to the box directions for two 9" cake pans.

4. Bake in preheated oven according to package instructions, until center of cake springs back when lightly touched.
Note: You will need only one round cake. Freeze the other cake for later use.

5. Beat egg whites with cream of tartar, salt, almond extract and sugar until stiff peaks form.

6. Line a baking sheet with parchment or heavy brown paper. Place cake in center. Turn molded ice cream out onto cake. Remove foil. Quickly and prettily spread meringue over cake and ice cream, all the way to paper to seal. Return to freezer 2 hours.

7. Preheat oven to 425 degrees.

8. Bake the Alaska on the lowest shelf, 8 to 10 minutes, or until meringue is lightly browned. Serve at once.

Fish and Meat

Oven Baked Salmon

Ingredients:

4 serving size pieces of salmon

Juice of one lemon

6-8 tablespoons mayonnaise

1 teaspoon dried dillweed

1/2 cup bread crumbs

2 tablespoon melted butter

Parsley for garnish

Directions:

1. Sprinkle each portion of fish with lemon juice.
2. Spread the top of each piece of salmon with about 1 to 2 tablespoons of mayonnaise.
3. Sprinkle with dill.
4. Sprinkle with bread crumbs.
5. Drizzle with melted butter.
6. Bake at 375 degrees in the oven uncovered for 25-35 minutes depending on the thickness of the fish.

Beef Wellington

Ingredients:

2-1/2 pound center cut beef tenderloins

1/2 teaspoon black pepper

1 egg

1 tablespoon water

1 tablespoon butter

2 cups finely chopped mushrooms

1 medium onion, finely chopped (about 1/2 cup)

2 tablespoons flour

1/2 of a 17.3 oz package Puff Pastry, 1 sheet, thawed

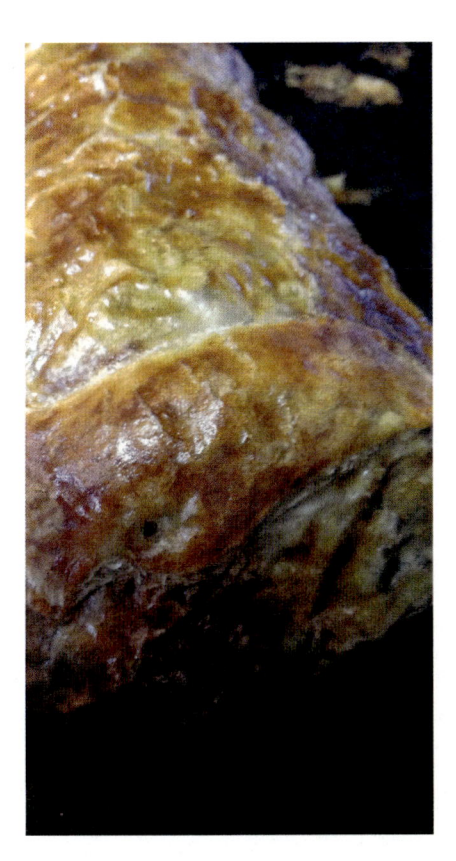

Directions:

1. Heat oven to 425 degrees.
2. Place the beef into a lightly greased roasting pan.
3. Season with black pepper.
4. Roast for 30 minutes or until a meat thermometer inserted into the beef reads 130 degrees.
5. Cover the pan and refrigerate for 1 hour.
6. Heat the butter in a 10 inch skillet over medium high heat.
7. Add mushrooms and onion and cook until the mushrooms are tender and all the liquid is evaporated, stirring often.
8. Sprinkle the work surface with the flour.
9. Unfold the pastry sheet on the work surface.
10. Roll the pastry sheet into a rectangle 4 inches longer and 6 inches wider than the beef.
11. Mix the egg and water together.
12. Brush pastry sheet with the egg mixture.
13. Spoon the mushroom mixture onto the pastry sheet to within 1- inch of the edge.
14. Place the beef in the center of the mushroom mixture.
15. Fold the pastry over the beef and press to seal.
16. Place seamside down onto a baking sheet.
17. Tuck the ends under to seal.
18. Brush the pastry with egg mixture.
19. Bake for 25 minutes or until pastry is golden brown and meat themometer reads 140 degrees.

Oven Beef Stew

Ingredients:

2-3 pounds chuck or round steak, cubed

2 cups celery, 1 inch pieces

2 cups carrots, 1 inch pieces

4 potatoes, 1 inch cubes

2 cups crushed tomatoes

2 cups water

2 tablespoons tapioca

1 package dry Lipton Soup Mix

1/4 teaspoon black pepper

Directions:

1. Combine all ingredients in a large casserole.
2. Seal completely in foil.
3. Place in oven at 275 degrees for 3 to 3-1/2 hours. Can be made in a slow cooker on low for 8 hours.

Note: You do not have to brown the beef before baking.

Luleh Kebab

Ingredients:

2-1/2 pounds lean ground beef

1 tablespoon tomato paste

4 oz tomato sauce

1 teaspoon pepper sauce

1 cup bread crumbs

4 tablespoons evaporated milk

1/4 cup minced parsley

1 tablespoon minced dried onion

1 teaspoon salt

1/4 teaspoon black pepper

Garnish:

1 cup minced onion

1/2 cup minced parsley

Directions:

1. Mix ingredients together and form into about 14 sausage shapes about 4 inches moistening hands with water as you shape.

2. Place kebabs in a shallow baking dish.

3. Bake 20 minutes in preheated 400 degree oven.

4. Transfer to a platter and reserve pan juices to serve separately.

5. Garnish kebabs with the chopped onion and parsley.

Sini Kufte

This dish has a top and bottom layer of meat with bulghar and a filling of ground meat, onions and spices.

Ingredients:

Filling:

2 pounds hamburger (85% lean)

1/2 pound butter,

2 pounds onions, chopped

1 teaspoon paprika

1/2 teaspoon allspice

1/2 teaspoon pepper

1 tablespoon salt

1/2 cup pine nuts or chopped walnuts

1/2 teaspoon basil

1/2 teaspoon cayenne pepper

Shell (top & bottom layers):

3 pounds top round meat, ground three times

2-1/2 cups fine bulghar

1-1/2 cups cold water (add more as needed)

3 teaspoon salt

3 teaspoons paprika

1/2 teaspoon pepper

1 cup hot broth

Directions

1. Butter one 12"x18" or two 9"x13" baking dishes.

Filling:

2. Melt 4 tablespoons butter in large skillet.
3. Saute meat and onions until the liquid from the meat is absorbed, 15 to 20 minutes and simmer a little longer.
4. Add seasonings and nuts, stir and cook 5 minutes and remove from heat.
5. Let cool, then refrigerate.

Shell (top and bottom layers):

6. Moisten bulghar with water, a little at a time.
7. Add remaining shell ingredients.
8. Knead for 15 -20 minutes until meat is smooth , moistening hands with water from time to time while kneading.
9. Layer 1/2 the shell mixture evenly in pan. (Roll between 2 sheets of wax paper to have a thin shell.)
10. Cover with filling mixture.
11. Roll a thin top shell and place over filling.
12. Wet hands to smooth the surface.
13. Spread remaining butter on top.
14. Cut into diamonds.
15. Spoon hot broth over surface and cover with aluminum foil.
16. Bake in preheated 375 degree oven for 1/2 hour and then remove foil.
17. Bake for another 30 minutes.

Gelatin Molds

Strawberry Gelatin Mold

Ingredients:

4 small (3 oz) packages strawberry gelatin

2 (10 oz.) packages frozen strawberries

1 (20 oz.) drained crushed pineapple

2 cups sour cream

4 cups boiling water

Directions:

1. Dissolve gelatin in boiling water.
2. Add frozen strawberries.
3. Stir until thawed.
4. Refrigerate until slightly gelled.
5. Add drained crushed pineapple.
6. Pour 1/2 of the mixture into oiled mold.
7. Set mold in refrigerator until firm. Keep remaining gelatin mixture on counter.
8. Remove from refrigerator and spread on sour cream.
9. Pour remaining gelatin mixture on top of sour cream.
10. Chill until firm.

Jellied Cranberry Mold

Ingredients:

2 small (3 oz) packages raspberry gelatin

1 cup boiling water

1 1/2 cups cold water

1 can (7 oz) mandarin oranges

1 (15 oz) can pineapple chunks, drain well

1 can (14 oz) whole cranberry sauce slightly beaten

1 cup chopped walnuts (optional)

Directions:

1. Dissolve gelatin in boiling water.
2. Add cold water and chill partially.
3. Cut mandarin oranges in half.
4. Cut pineapple chunks in half.
5. Fold oranges, pineapple, cranberry, nuts into gelatin. Pour into mold and refrigerate overnight.

Mandarin Orange Salad

Ingredients:

4 small (3 oz) packages orange gelatin

4 cups boiling water

1 quart orange sherbet

1 can (15 oz) crushed pineapple, drained

2 small (7 oz) cans Mandarin oranges, drained

Directions:

1. Dissolve 4 packages of gelatin powder in 4 cups boiling water.
2. Fold in sherbet.
3. Partially set in refrigerator until gelled about 45 minutes to 1 hour.
4. Remove from refrigerator and add pineapple and Mandarin oranges.
5. Pour into an oiled bundt pan and set overnight in refrigerator.
6. Unmold and serve.

Miscellaneous

Grilled Cheese Sandwich

Ingredients:

2 teaspoons vegetable oil

1 large onion, thinly sliced into half moons (about 2 cups)

Pinch of cayenne pepper

8 thin slices Wisconsin Brick cheese (about 6 oz)

8 slices whole-wheat sandwich bread

1 large or 2 medium ripe beefsteak or hothouse tomatoes, sliced

Cooking Spray

Directions:

1. Heat the oil in a medium nonstick skillet over medium high heat.

2. Reduce the heat to medium-low, add the onion, cover and cook, stirring occasionally, until the onions are golden, about 10 minutes.

3. Remove the lid and cook, uncovered, stirring frequently until the onions are golden brown and the edges are browned, 10 to 12 additional minutes.

4. Stir in the cayenne pepper. (Onions may be made up to 3 days ahead and stored in the refrigerator.)

5. Place one slice of brick cheese on each of 4 slices of the bread.

6. Spread a quarter (about 2 tablespoons.) of the caramelized onions on top, then place one large or 2 medium slices tomato.

7. Place another slice of cheese on top of that, then the other slice of bread.

8. Place sandwich on medium-high heat on a grill sprayed with cooking spray.

9. Lower the heat to medium-low and grill until the underside is a deep brown and the cheese is partially melted, 3 to 4 minutes.

10. Flip the sandwich and grill the other side, another 3 minutes.

11. Slice in half and serve hot.

Pineapple Bread Stuffing

Ingredients:

4 eggs

1/2 cup sugar

1/3 cup butter

1 can (20 oz) crushed pineapple, drained

5 slices white bread, cubed

Directions

1. Beat eggs.
2. Add sugar, butter and drained pineapple.
3. Fold in bread cubes.
4. Spread in 7"x11" greased baking dish.
5. Bake 350 degrees for 45 minutes or until top is brown.

Strawberry Jam á la Jim

Ingredients:

5 cups prepared fruit (buy about 2 quarts of fully ripe strawberries)

1 box Sure-Jell Fruit Pectin

1/2 teaspoon butter or margarine

7 cups sugar, measured into separate bowl

Direction:

1. Wash jars and screw bands in hot soapy water; rinse with warm water. Pour boiling water over flat lids in saucepan off the heat. Let stand in hot water until ready to use. Drain well before filling.

2. Stem and crush strawberries or process slightly. Measure exactly 5 cups prepared fruit into 6 or 8 qt. saucepot.

3. Stir pectin into fruit in saucepot. Add butter to reduce foaming. Bring mixture to full rolling boil (a boil that doesn't stop bubbling when stirred) on high heat, stirring constantly. Stir in sugar. Return to full rolling boil and boil exactly 1 min., stirring constantly. Remove from heat. Skim off any foam with metal spoon.

4. Ladle immediately into prepared jars, filling to within 1 inch of tops. Wipe jar rims and threads. Cover with two-piece lids. Screw bands tightly. Invert and let cool. Store in refrigerator or freezer. This jam is even better than Smucker's!

Pilafs and Pastas

Cheese Noodle Dish

Ingredients:

1/2 lb Cheddar and 1/2 lb Muenster

1 package 1/2 to 3/4 inch egg noodles

1/2 stick melted butter

2 tablespoon chopped parsley

3 eggs, beaten

1/2 cup milk

Directions:

1. Boil noodles in salted water until tender. Drain and rinse with cold water. Add the melted butter and 1 tablespoon chopped parsley to the noodles.

2. Place half of the noodles in a buttered 9 x 13 baking dish.

3. Sprinkle the grated cheese on the noodles. Reserve some cheese to sprinkle on the top.

4. Make another layer of the remaining noodles.

5. Beat 3 eggs in a bowl with milk and pour over the pan. Sprinkle reserved cheese.

6. Bake uncovered in 350 degree oven for 30 to 40 minutes. Garnish with remaining parsley.

Bulghar Pilaf with Onions

Ingredients:

2 tablespoons olive oil

1/2 cup chopped onions

1/3 cup fine egg noodles

1 cup cracked wheat (medium-coarse or coarse bulghar, #3)

2 cups hot chicken broth

4 tablespoons butter

1/2 teaspoon salt

1/4 teaspoon black pepper

Directions:

1. Melt shortening in a 2 quart saucepan and add onions.

2. Saute gently, and add in the fine egg noodles stirring with a fork to brown evenly.

3. Add wheat and stir to mix.

4. Pour in broth, butter and seasonings.

5. Bring to a boil, cover and simmer 15 minutes, or until liquid is absorbed.

6. Keep covered, remove from heat and let rest for 10 minutes

Note: Bulghar is cracked wheat that has been steamed partially, like oatmeal, but cracked wheat is the raw non cooked product so it may take longer to cook.

Rice Pilaf

Ingredients:

1 cup rice (Uncle Ben's)

1/4 cup fine egg noodles

2-1/2 cups chicken broth

1/2 stick of butter

salt and pepper

Directions:

1. Melt butter in a shallow pan.

2. Break up fine egg noodles and fry in butter until slightly browned, stirring constantly.

3. Wash and drain the rice well, then add to the fine egg noodles and saute them together for a few minutes, always stirring.

4. Add the hot broth and water and add salt and pepper.

5. Cover and cook on low for 20 minutes until all the broth is absorbed.

6. Let rest 15 minutes. Give it another stir with a fork and serve hot.

A meal of chicken & pilaf is a favorite at Armenian Church dinners everywhere!

Salads

Spinach/Arugula Salad á la Shirley

Dressing Ingredients:

1/2 cup whole cranberry sauce

1/4 cup vegetable oil

2 tablespoons orange juice

2 tablespoons honey

2 tablespoon Balsamic vinegar

1/4 teaspoons salt

Salad Ingredients:

1 bag baby spinach

arugula (any amount)

2 avocados, sliced thin

2 tablespoons orange juice to coat the avocado

1/2 cup pomegranate seeds

Note: Cut pomegranate and place in cold water - seeds come out easily.

Dried cranberries can be used in place of the pomegranate seeds.

Directions:

1. Combine all ingredients for dressing in a small bowl. Whisk well.

2. Combine salad greens in a large bowl. Slice avocado and drizzle with the orange juice, coating the avocado well.

3. Drizzle as much dressing as you desire over salad.

4. Toss well. Sprinkle with pomegranate seeds or dried cranberries.

Strawberry Spinach Salad

Ingredients:

2 tablespoons sesame seeds

1 tablespoon poppy seeds

1/2 cup white sugar

1/2 cup olive oil

1/4 cup white vinegar

1/4 teaspoon paprika

1/4 teaspoon Worchestershire sauce

1 tablespoon minced onion

10 oz fresh spinach, rinsed, dried, torn into bite-size pieces.

1 quart strawberries, cleaned, hulled and sliced

1/4 cup almonds, blanched and slivered

Directions:

1. In a medium bowl whisk sesame seeds, poppy seeds, sugar, olive oil, vinegar, paprika, Worchestershire sauce and onion.

2. Cover and chill one hour.

3. In a large bowl, combine spinach, strawberries and almonds.

4. Pour dressing over salad and toss.

5. Refrigerate 10 to 15 minutes before serving.

Baked Grapefruit Alaska

Ingredients:

3 medium grapefruit

1 jar grapefruit sections

1 (10 oz) jar orange marmalade

4 to 6 egg whites, room temperature

Powdered sugar

Directions:

1. Cut each grapefruit in half.
2. With grapefruit knife remove center core from each half.
3. Detach flesh from shell leaving flesh in grapefruit sections.
4. Add extra grapefruit from jar.
5. Place on a baking sheet.
6. Warm marmalade.
7. In a medium bowl, beat egg whites until soft peaks form.
8. Slowly beat in granulated sugar 1 tablespoon at a time.
9. Continue beating until stiff.
10. Carefully fold in warm marmalade.
11. Cover grapefruit in shells with meringue, bringing meringue to the edge of the shells. Filled shells may stand at room temperature 2-3 hours until ready to use.
12. Just before serving, preheat oven to 425 degrees. Place grapefruit in oven for 8 to 9 minutes until browned.
13. Sprinkle with powdered sugar and serve immediately.

Tomato Salad

Dressing Ingredients:

2 large onions, quartered and sliced thin

4 large ripe tomatoes, quartered and sliced

1-1/2 teaspoons salt

1/4 teaspoon black pepper

1/4 cup minced parsley

4 tablespoons olive oil

3 tablespoons lemon juice

Directions:

1. Mix together onions and 1 teaspoon salt.
2. Squeeze onions and rinse in cold water.
3. Squeeze again until fairly dry and combine with tomatoes.
4. Add 1/2 teaspoon salt, pepper, parsley and olive oil. Do not add lemon juice yet.
5. Refrigerate at least 1 hour before serving.
6. Add lemon juice just before serving.

Tropical Salad Bowl

Salad Ingredients:

2 heads romaine lettuce

1 head Bibb lettuce

1 papaya

Papaya Seed Dressing, see below

1 large avocado

Papaya Seed Dressing Ingredients:

1/2 cup sugar

2 teaspoons salt

1/2 teaspoon dry mustard

1/2 cup white vinegar

1/2 cup vegetable oil

1/2 cup chopped onion

2 tablespoons fresh papaya seeds

Directions:

1. Wash lettuce and shake off excess water. Tear into bite-size pieces. Wrap in paper towels, place in a plastic bag and refrigerate overnight to crisp.

2. Before serving salad, place lettuce in large bowl.

3. Peel and slice papaya, reserving 2 tablespoons seeds for dressing.

4. Prepare Papaya Seed Salad Dressing.

   - Places all ingredients except papaya seeds into blender or food processor fitted with the metal blade.
   - Blend; add papaya seeds and process only until they are the size of coarsely ground black paper.
   - May be refrigerated up to 3 days. Peel and slice avocado.

5. Add papaya and avocado to greens and toss with salad dressing.

Soups

Red Lentil Soup

Also known as Kyle's Soup!

Ingredients:

2 cups red lentils

3/4 cup medium grain rice

8 - 10 cups chicken broth

1 chopped onion

3 tablespoons catsup

1 tablespoon red pepper sauce

1/2 stick butter

1 teaspoon crushed dried mint

1 teaspoon salt

Black pepper

Directions:

1. Combine the lentils, rice, broth and onion. Simmer 20 minutes.

2. Add in catsup and red pepper sauce.

3. In another pot melt butter and stir in dried mint and salt. Sprinkle with black pepper.

4. Combine everything and add more broth if needed.

Lemon Egg Soup

Ingredients:

4 cups chicken broth

1 cup fine egg noodles

1 teaspoon salt

2 eggs

Juice of 1 lemon

Option: chunks of cooked chicken maybe added

Directions:

1. Bring broth to boil.

2. Add noodles and cook about 15 minutes.

3. Beat eggs until light and frothy.

4. Gradually stir in lemon juice to eggs.

5. Slowly spoon about 2 cup of hot broth into egg mixture, tempering the mixture.

6. Slowly pour into soup and simmer about 1 minute.

7. Garnish with parsley (optional)

Roasted Chicken Soup

Ingredients:

1 tablespoon vegetable oil

2 medium onions, cut in half and thinly sliced

8 cups chicken broth

1/4 teaspoon ground black pepper and 1 teaspoon salt

2 medium carrots, sliced

2 stalks celery, sliced

3/4 cup uncooked pasta (trumpet shaped or other small pasta)

2 cups roasted chicken cut into strips

Directions:

1. Heat oil in large skillet over medium-high heat.

2. Add onions and cook until they begin to brown, stirring occasionally.

3. Reduce heat to medium and cook until onions are tender and caramelized, stirring occasionally. Remove from heat.

4. Heat broth, black pepper, carrots and celery in saucepan over medium high heat to a boil.

5. Stir pasta and chicken in saucepan.

6. Reduce heat to medium and cook 10 minutes or until pasta is tender.

7. Stir in onions and serve.

Butternut Squash Soup

Ingredients:

6 tablespoons chopped onion

4 tablespoons butter

6 cups peeled and cubed butternut squash

3 cups chicken broth

1/2 teaspoon dried marjoram

3/4 teaspoon ground black pepper

1/4 teaspoon ground cayenne pepper

1 (8 oz) package cream cheese

Directions:

1. In a large saucepan, saute onions in butter until tender. Add squash, chicken broth, marjoram, black pepper and cayenne pepper.

2. Bring to a boil and cook 20 minutes or until squash is tender.

3. Puree mixture and cream cheese in a food processor in batches until smooth.

Yogurt Noodle Soup

Ingredients:

4 cups chicken broth

1 teaspoon salt

2 cups 1/4 inch wide noodles

4 tablespoons butter

1 large onion, minced

2 cups yogurt

1 tablespoon flour

1 egg

1 tablespoon crushed dried mint

Directions:

1. Bring chicken broth to a boil and add salt.

2. Add noodles and simmer for 10 minutes or until noodles are tender.

3. Melt butter in a skillet and saute onions until golden brown, about 10 minutes. Stir in mint. Keep warm over low heat.

4. In a separate bowl, beat together yogurt, flour, and egg for 3 minutes with a rotary beater.

5. Warm the yogurt mixture by adding a few spoonfuls of the broth to the yogurt a little at a time, tempering the mixture.

6. When yogurt is warmed gradually pour it into the broth while stirring.

7. Add mint and onions, stir and serve.

Vegetables

Green Beans with Lamb

Ingredients:

2 pounds lamb stew, cut small

4 tablespoons butter

2 pounds trimmed, fresh green beans

2 onions, halved and sliced

1/2 teaspoon salt

1/4 teaspoon black pepper

1 crushed clove of garlic

2 tablespoon chopped dill

1 tablespoon tomato paste

1 teaspoon pepper paste

1 can (8 oz) tomato sauce

1 cup water or broth

Directions:

1. Braise meet in melted butter 10 to 15 minutes, browning evenly.

2. Combine beans, onions, and seasoning and add to the meat.

3. Combine tomato paste, sauce, pepper paste and water or broth and add to meat.

4. Bring to a boil, lower heat and simmer, covered for 1-1/2 to 2 hours or until beans are tender.

Green Beans with Olive Oil

Ingredients:

1 1/2 pounds fresh green beans

1-1/2 cups water

1/2 cup tomato sauce

1 teaspoon tomato paste

1/2 teaspoon mild pepper paste

1/3 cup olive oil

1 medium onion, chopped

1 teaspoon salt

1/8 teaspoon black pepper

Directions:

1. Wash, trim and cut green beans or leave whole.

2. Boil water and add green beans and onion.

3. When half tender add remaining ingredients and simmer until tender.

Fresh Mushroom Casserole

Ingredients:

1 pound fresh mushrooms

1/4 cup butter or margarine

2 beef bouillon cubes

1/2 cup hot water

2 tablespoon flour

1/2 cup half and half cream

dash of salt

dash of pepper

1/2 to 1 cup grated Parmesan cheese

1/2 cup bread crumbs

Directions:

1. Clean mushrooms and slice off ends.
2. Place in buttered 1-quart casserole. Set aside.
3. Melt butter and bouillon cubes in hot water.
4. Blend in flour, cream, salt and pepper.
5. Pour over mushrooms.
6. Mix cheese and bread crumbs, add to mushrooms and toss gently.
7. Bake uncovered at 350 degrees for approximately 30 minutes.

Squash/Rice Dish

Ingredients:

1 butternut squash, cut in 1/4" rounds

1 cup medium grain rice

2-1/2 cups water

1/2 stick butter (1/4 cup) plus 2 tablespoons

6 tablespoons brown sugar

6 tablespoons Maple Syrup

2 tablespoons water

1 tablespoon sugar

1 teaspoon salt

Directions:

1. Bring 2-1/2 cups water to a boil.
2. Add rice, 1 tablespoon sugar and 1 teaspoon salt, cover and cook on simmer for 10 minutes.
3. Butter the bottom and sides of a "9 x 13" pan.
4. Layer squash on first layer, rice on second layer, then dot with 1/2 stick butter.
5. Add another layer of squash.
6. Sprinkle with brown sugar, maple syrup, 2 tablespoons melted butter, and 2 tablespoons water.
   Note: Photo shows dish before baking
7. Cover with foil and bake 45 minutes at 400 degrees, uncover and bake 15 minutes at 375 degrees.

Liz Derderian . . .

My mom is not only an incredible cook, but she is an amazing host, making everyone feel welcome.

Similar to my dad's carriage house, my mom's kitchen is filled with tools, all precisely arranged in their perfect location. Dishes are stacked, facing forward, and never out of place. It is hard to tell if her dishwasher is clean or dirty.

Preparing food and giving to others is part of my mom's DNA. She excitedly prepares lists weeks before hosting a summer cookout. She happily spends hours preparing perfect paklava. She eagerly awaits visitors, those planned and unplanned, and, thanks to multiple large freezers, always has something delicious to serve at a moment's notice. She loves having a house full of guests over the holidays.

Over the years she has designed elaborate birthday parties, church gatherings, school events and dinner parties. She has graciously hosted friends from other countries, some who don't speak her language, and she does it all beautifully and with a smile. She makes everyone feel like they are home.

Mom's holiday celebrations are flawless. Candelabras. Crystal. Invitations for everyone to be included. The kids are allowed to enter the dinner room only when the table is set. However, I think it is her everyday meals that stand out in my memory because she brings the same flawless preparation, which I never truly appreciated until I was an adult.

A casual breakfast has multiple courses, and everything is homemade. She serves choreg, muffins and basturma that may have been cured over a few weeks, hanging in the garage, wafting spices into the house. Puff pancakes with strawberries and powdered sugar for her three smiling grandchildren are a favorite. The table is set for lunch, too, even if you are simply coming in from the pool on a hot summer day. The table is likely filled with recently picked vegetables from the yard, or maybe, if you're lucky, blueberries are laid out on industrial-size trays. There are also "regular" family dinners that may consist of my favorite Armenian dish, lamb and green beans (which takes all day to prepare). I'll never forget having soup delivered within an hour of casually mentioning to my mom that I had a little scratch in my throat. It brings her joy to do things for others.

We all have our favorite dishes. For Julie, it is the Tropical Salad Bowl, page 64; Abigail, the Eetch, page 11; and Kyle enjoys "Kyle Soup" (Lentil Soup, page 66). At Grandma's house there is always room for dessert (and no limits). By the young age of 3, my children learned where to "steal" a bag of frozen choereg, Grandma's specialty.

My mom's kitchen is magical. For most humans, it takes a few days to recover from hosting a party. For my mom, there is never a sign of it the next day. She works from a meticulously detailed menu and list. Serving dishes are labeled with a post-it note. Nothing is missed, and on the very rare occasion when something goes awry (the Thanksgiving the turkey took too long to cook, the time the Jello mold was forgotten in the outdoor refrigerator or the Christmas when the chestnuts popped all over the kitchen), it becomes part of our family folklore.

Jim and Liz Derderian with Bethany, Christian and Alison

I have developed my love of cooking from my mother. I continue to admire her example of how to properly host friends and family and show you care for them through an invitation and a beautiful meal. I love setting the table the day before. I believe you can never have enough glassware, and I always follow her formula for creating conversation by mixing couples in the seating arrangement.

We are all grateful to you, Mom, for sharing your passion for cooking, for bringing our family together and for making us always feel like we are home.

Christian Derderian

Planning a Dinner Party

Choose TIME and DATE

Compile a GUEST LIST

Contact Guests with an INVITATION

Plan MENU

APPETIZERS

Name

Ingredients Needed

Day, Time for Cooking or Baking

Serving Pieces

Placement

Utensils

BAR SETUP/BEVERAGES

Name

Items Needed

Serving Pieces

Placement

Utensils

DINNER

Name

Ingredients Needed

Day, Time for Cooking or Baking

Serving Pieces

Placement

Utensils

DESSERTS

Name

Ingredients Needed

Day, Time for Cooking or Baking

Serving Pieces

Placement

Utensils

COFFEE, Tea, etc.

Items Needed

Time of Preparation

Serving Pieces

Placement

Utensils

TABLE "DECOR"

CANDLES

CENTERPIECE

TABLECLOTH & NAPKINS

DINNERWARE

PLACE CARDS

SPECIAL "TREATS"

SEATING ARRANGEMENT

Table set for buffet style dinner.

Vartuhy's Legacy

Vartuhy had seven children, daughters Catherine, Mary, Rose, Margaret and Elizabeth and sons Jack and Michael. There were 14 grandchildren, 20 greatgrandchildren, and two great-great grandchildren. In the summer of 2016, many of them gathered to revitalize her rock garden with mosaics on the front and back of the wall, new rocks and new plants. This is great-great grandson Hudson. It was a creative and joyful time!

The cover design of this cookbook came from the sign for Vartuhy's Garden, by Alison Derderian.

Another legacy is Grandpa Toros's water fountain that stands in the Wustum Museum Rose Garden.

Manufactured by Amazon.ca
Bolton, ON